- PROJECT NAME
- PROJECT TYPE ☐ CLOTHING ☐ H(
- SEWING PATTERN
- M
- STARTED
- FINISHED

SET-UP

- MACHINE
- SETTINGS
- NEEDLE USED
- THREAD USED

SKETCH

MEASUREMENT

MATERIALS

ITEM	QUANTITY	PRICE
☐		
☐		
☐		
☐		
☐		

PROJECT NAME	
PROJECT TYPE ☐ CLOTHING ☐ HOME DECOR ☐ OTHER	
SEWING PATTERN	MADE FOR
STARTED	FINISHED

SET-UP

MACHINE
SETTINGS
NEEDLE USED
THREAD USED

SKETCH

MEASUREMENT

MATERIALS

ITEM	QUANTITY	PRICE
☐		
☐		
☐		
☐		
☐		

PROJECT NAME

PROJECT TYPE ☐ CLOTHING ☐ HOME DECOR ☐ OTHER

SEWING PATTERN | **MADE FOR**

STARTED | **FINISHED**

SET-UP

- MACHINE
- SETTINGS
- NEEDLE USED
- THREAD USED

SKETCH

MEASUREMENT

MATERIALS

ITEM	QUANTITY	PRICE
☐		
☐		
☐		
☐		
☐		

PROJECT NAME	
PROJECT TYPE ☐ CLOTHING ☐ HOME DECOR ☐ OTHER	
SEWING PATTERN	MADE FOR
STARTED	FINISHED

SET-UP

- MACHINE
- SETTINGS
- NEEDLE USED
- THREAD USED

SKETCH

MEASUREMENT

MATERIALS

ITEM	QUANTITY	PRICE
☐		
☐		
☐		
☐		
☐		

PROJECT NAME

PROJECT TYPE ☐ CLOTHING ☐ HOME DECOR ☐ OTHER

SEWING PATTERN | **MADE FOR**

STARTED | **FINISHED**

SET-UP

- MACHINE
- SETTINGS
- NEEDLE USED
- THREAD USED

SKETCH

MEASUREMENT

MATERIALS

ITEM	QUANTITY	PRICE
☐		
☐		
☐		
☐		
☐		

PROJECT NAME	
PROJECT TYPE ☐ CLOTHING ☐ HOME DECOR ☐ OTHER	
SEWING PATTERN	MADE FOR
STARTED	FINISHED

SET-UP

- MACHINE
- SETTINGS
- NEEDLE USED
- THREAD USED

SKETCH

MEASUREMENT

MATERIALS

ITEM	QUANTITY	PRICE
☐		
☐		
☐		
☐		
☐		

PROJECT NAME	
PROJECT TYPE ☐ CLOTHING ☐ HOME DECOR ☐ OTHER	
SEWING PATTERN	MADE FOR
STARTED	FINISHED

SET-UP

- MACHINE
- SETTINGS
-
- NEEDLE USED
- THREAD USED

SKETCH

MEASUREMENT

MATERIALS

ITEM	QUANTITY	PRICE
☐		
☐		
☐		
☐		
☐		

PROJECT NAME	
PROJECT TYPE ☐ CLOTHING ☐ HOME DECOR ☐ OTHER	
SEWING PATTERN	MADE FOR
STARTED	FINISHED

SET-UP

- MACHINE
- SETTINGS
- NEEDLE USED
- THREAD USED

SKETCH

MEASUREMENT

MATERIALS

ITEM	QUANTITY	PRICE
☐		
☐		
☐		
☐		
☐		

PROJECT NAME					
PROJECT TYPE	☐ CLOTHING		☐ HOME DECOR		☐ OTHER
SEWING PATTERN			MADE FOR		
STARTED			FINISHED		

SET-UP	SKETCH
MACHINE	
SETTINGS	
NEEDLE USED	
THREAD USED	

MEASUREMENT

MATERIALS

ITEM	QUANTITY	PRICE
☐		
☐		
☐		
☐		
☐		

PROJECT NAME	
PROJECT TYPE ☐ CLOTHING ☐ HOME DECOR ☐ OTHER	
SEWING PATTERN	MADE FOR
STARTED	FINISHED

SET-UP

- MACHINE
- SETTINGS
- NEEDLE USED
- THREAD USED

MEASUREMENT

SKETCH

MATERIALS

ITEM	QUANTITY	PRICE
☐		
☐		
☐		
☐		
☐		

PROJECT NAME	
PROJECT TYPE ☐ CLOTHING ☐ HOME DECOR ☐ OTHER	
SEWING PATTERN	MADE FOR
STARTED	FINISHED

SET-UP

- MACHINE
- SETTINGS
- NEEDLE USED
- THREAD USED

SKETCH

MEASUREMENT

MATERIALS

ITEM	QUANTITY	PRICE
☐		
☐		
☐		
☐		
☐		

- **PROJECT NAME**
- **PROJECT TYPE** ☐ CLOTHING ☐ HOME DECOR ☐ OTHER
- **SEWING PATTERN**
- **MADE FOR**
- **STARTED**
- **FINISHED**

SET-UP
- MACHINE
- SETTINGS
- NEEDLE USED
- THREAD USED

SKETCH

MEASUREMENT

MATERIALS

ITEM	QUANTITY	PRICE
☐		
☐		
☐		
☐		
☐		

PROJECT NAME	
PROJECT TYPE ☐ CLOTHING ☐ HOME DECOR ☐ OTHER	
SEWING PATTERN	MADE FOR
STARTED	FINISHED

SET-UP

- MACHINE
- SETTINGS
- NEEDLE USED
- THREAD USED

SKETCH

MEASUREMENT

MATERIALS

ITEM	QUANTITY	PRICE
☐		
☐		
☐		
☐		
☐		

PROJECT NAME					
PROJECT TYPE	☐ CLOTHING		☐ HOME DECOR		☐ OTHER
SEWING PATTERN			**MADE FOR**		
STARTED			**FINISHED**		

SET-UP

- MACHINE
- SETTINGS
- NEEDLE USED
- THREAD USED

SKETCH

MEASUREMENT

MATERIALS

ITEM	QUANTITY	PRICE
☐		
☐		
☐		
☐		
☐		

PROJECT NAME

PROJECT TYPE ☐ CLOTHING   ☐ HOME DECOR   ☐ OTHER

SEWING PATTERN | **MADE FOR**

STARTED | **FINISHED**

SET-UP

- MACHINE
- SETTINGS
- NEEDLE USED
- THREAD USED

SKETCH

MEASUREMENT

MATERIALS

ITEM	QUANTITY	PRICE
☐		
☐		
☐		
☐		
☐		

PROJECT NAME	
PROJECT TYPE	☐ CLOTHING ☐ HOME DECOR ☐ OTHER
SEWING PATTERN	MADE FOR
STARTED	FINISHED

SET-UP

MACHINE	
SETTINGS	
NEEDLE USED	
THREAD USED	

SKETCH

MEASUREMENT

MATERIALS

ITEM	QUANTITY	PRICE
☐		
☐		
☐		
☐		
☐		

PROJECT NAME	
PROJECT TYPE ☐ CLOTHING ☐ HOME DECOR ☐ OTHER	
SEWING PATTERN	MADE FOR
STARTED	FINISHED

SET-UP

- MACHINE
- SETTINGS
-
- NEEDLE USED
- THREAD USED

SKETCH

MEASUREMENT

MATERIALS

ITEM	QUANTITY	PRICE
☐		
☐		
☐		
☐		
☐		

PROJECT NAME	
PROJECT TYPE ☐ CLOTHING ☐ HOME DECOR ☐ OTHER	
SEWING PATTERN	MADE FOR
STARTED	FINISHED

SET-UP

- MACHINE
- SETTINGS
- NEEDLE USED
- THREAD USED

SKETCH

MEASUREMENT

MATERIALS

ITEM	QUANTITY	PRICE
☐		
☐		
☐		
☐		
☐		

PROJECT NAME	
PROJECT TYPE ☐ CLOTHING ☐ HOME DECOR ☐ OTHER	
SEWING PATTERN	MADE FOR
STARTED	FINISHED

SET-UP

- MACHINE
- SETTINGS
-
- NEEDLE USED
- THREAD USED

SKETCH

MEASUREMENT

MATERIALS

ITEM	QUANTITY	PRICE
☐		
☐		
☐		
☐		
☐		

- PROJECT NAME
- PROJECT TYPE   ☐ CLOTHING   ☐ HOME DECOR   ☐ OTHER
- SEWING PATTERN
- MADE FOR
- STARTED
- FINISHED

SET-UP

- MACHINE
- SETTINGS
- NEEDLE USED
- THREAD USED

SKETCH

MEASUREMENT

MATERIALS

ITEM	QUANTITY	PRICE
☐		
☐		
☐		
☐		
☐		

PROJECT NAME	

PROJECT TYPE	☐ CLOTHING		☐ HOME DECOR		☐ OTHER

SEWING PATTERN		MADE FOR	
STARTED		FINISHED	

SET-UP

- MACHINE
- SETTINGS
- NEEDLE USED
- THREAD USED

SKETCH

MEASUREMENT

MATERIALS

ITEM	QUANTITY	PRICE
☐		
☐		
☐		
☐		
☐		

PROJECT NAME	
PROJECT TYPE ☐ CLOTHING ☐ HOME DECOR ☐ OTHER	
SEWING PATTERN	MADE FOR
STARTED	FINISHED

SET-UP

- MACHINE
- SETTINGS
-
- NEEDLE USED
- THREAD USED

SKETCH

MEASUREMENT

MATERIALS

ITEM	QUANTITY	PRICE
☐		
☐		
☐		
☐		
☐		

- **PROJECT NAME**
- **PROJECT TYPE** ☐ CLOTHING   ☐ HOME DECOR   ☐ OTHER
- **SEWING PATTERN**
- **MADE FOR**
- **STARTED**
- **FINISHED**

SET-UP

- MACHINE
- SETTINGS
- NEEDLE USED
- THREAD USED

SKETCH

MEASUREMENT

MATERIALS

ITEM	QUANTITY	PRICE
☐		
☐		
☐		
☐		
☐		

PROJECT NAME	
PROJECT TYPE ☐ CLOTHING ☐ HOME DECOR ☐ OTHER	
SEWING PATTERN	MADE FOR
STARTED	FINISHED

SET-UP

- MACHINE
- SETTINGS
- NEEDLE USED
- THREAD USED

SKETCH

MEASUREMENT

MATERIALS

ITEM	QUANTITY	PRICE
☐		
☐		
☐		
☐		
☐		

PROJECT NAME

PROJECT TYPE ☐ CLOTHING   ☐ HOME DECOR   ☐ OTHER

SEWING PATTERN

MADE FOR

STARTED

FINISHED

SET-UP

- MACHINE
- SETTINGS
- NEEDLE USED
- THREAD USED

SKETCH

MEASUREMENT

MATERIALS

ITEM	QUANTITY	PRICE
☐		
☐		
☐		
☐		
☐		

PROJECT NAME	
PROJECT TYPE ☐ CLOTHING ☐ HOME DECOR ☐ OTHER	
SEWING PATTERN	MADE FOR
STARTED	FINISHED

SET-UP

- MACHINE
- SETTINGS
- NEEDLE USED
- THREAD USED

SKETCH

MEASUREMENT

MATERIALS

ITEM	QUANTITY	PRICE
☐		
☐		
☐		
☐		
☐		

PROJECT NAME

PROJECT TYPE ☐ CLOTHING ☐ HOME DECOR ☐ OTHER

SEWING PATTERN

MADE FOR

STARTED

FINISHED

SET-UP

- MACHINE
- SETTINGS
- NEEDLE USED
- THREAD USED

SKETCH

MEASUREMENT

MATERIALS

ITEM	QUANTITY	PRICE
☐		
☐		
☐		
☐		
☐		

PROJECT NAME	
PROJECT TYPE ☐ CLOTHING ☐ HOME DECOR ☐ OTHER	
SEWING PATTERN	MADE FOR
STARTED	FINISHED

SET-UP

- MACHINE
- SETTINGS
-
- NEEDLE USED
- THREAD USED

SKETCH

MEASUREMENT

MATERIALS

ITEM	QUANTITY	PRICE
☐		
☐		
☐		
☐		
☐		

PROJECT NAME

PROJECT TYPE ☐ CLOTHING   ☐ HOME DECOR   ☐ OTHER

SEWING PATTERN

MADE FOR

STARTED

FINISHED

SET-UP

- MACHINE
- SETTINGS
- NEEDLE USED
- THREAD USED

SKETCH

MEASUREMENT

MATERIALS

ITEM	QUANTITY	PRICE
☐		
☐		
☐		
☐		
☐		

PROJECT NAME	
PROJECT TYPE ☐ CLOTHING ☐ HOME DECOR ☐ OTHER	
SEWING PATTERN	MADE FOR
STARTED	FINISHED

SET-UP

- MACHINE
- SETTINGS
-
- NEEDLE USED
- THREAD USED

SKETCH

MEASUREMENT

MATERIALS

ITEM	QUANTITY	PRICE
☐		
☐		
☐		
☐		
☐		

PROJECT NAME	
PROJECT TYPE	☐ CLOTHING ☐ HOME DECOR ☐ OTHER
SEWING PATTERN	MADE FOR
STARTED	FINISHED

SET-UP

- MACHINE
- SETTINGS
- NEEDLE USED
- THREAD USED

SKETCH

MEASUREMENT

MATERIALS

ITEM	QUANTITY	PRICE
☐		
☐		
☐		
☐		
☐		

PROJECT NAME	
PROJECT TYPE ☐ CLOTHING ☐ HOME DECOR ☐ OTHER	
SEWING PATTERN	MADE FOR
STARTED	FINISHED

SET-UP

- MACHINE
- SETTINGS
- NEEDLE USED
- THREAD USED

SKETCH

MEASUREMENT

MATERIALS

ITEM	QUANTITY	PRICE
☐		
☐		
☐		
☐		
☐		

PROJECT NAME

PROJECT TYPE ☐ CLOTHING ☐ HOME DECOR ☐ OTHER

SEWING PATTERN

MADE FOR

STARTED

FINISHED

SET-UP

MACHINE	
SETTINGS	
NEEDLE USED	
THREAD USED	

SKETCH

MEASUREMENT

MATERIALS

ITEM	QUANTITY	PRICE
☐		
☐		
☐		
☐		
☐		

PROJECT NAME	
PROJECT TYPE ☐ CLOTHING ☐ HOME DECOR ☐ OTHER	
SEWING PATTERN	MADE FOR
STARTED	FINISHED

SET-UP

- MACHINE
- SETTINGS
- NEEDLE USED
- THREAD USED

SKETCH

MEASUREMENT

MATERIALS

ITEM	QUANTITY	PRICE
☐		
☐		
☐		
☐		
☐		

PROJECT NAME	
PROJECT TYPE ☐ CLOTHING ☐ HOME DECOR ☐ OTHER	
SEWING PATTERN	MADE FOR
STARTED	FINISHED

SET-UP

- MACHINE
- SETTINGS
- NEEDLE USED
- THREAD USED

SKETCH

MEASUREMENT

MATERIALS

ITEM	QUANTITY	PRICE
☐		
☐		
☐		
☐		
☐		

PROJECT NAME	
PROJECT TYPE ☐ CLOTHING ☐ HOME DECOR ☐ OTHER	
SEWING PATTERN	MADE FOR
STARTED	FINISHED

SET-UP

- MACHINE
- SETTINGS
- NEEDLE USED
- THREAD USED

SKETCH

MEASUREMENT

MATERIALS

ITEM	QUANTITY	PRICE
☐		
☐		
☐		
☐		
☐		

PROJECT NAME

PROJECT TYPE ☐ CLOTHING ☐ HOME DECOR ☐ OTHER

SEWING PATTERN

MADE FOR

STARTED

FINISHED

SET-UP

MACHINE

SETTINGS

NEEDLE USED

THREAD USED

SKETCH

MEASUREMENT

MATERIALS

ITEM	QUANTITY	PRICE
☐		
☐		
☐		
☐		
☐		

PROJECT NAME	
PROJECT TYPE ☐ CLOTHING ☐ HOME DECOR ☐ OTHER	
SEWING PATTERN	MADE FOR
STARTED	FINISHED

SET-UP

- MACHINE
- SETTINGS
- NEEDLE USED
- THREAD USED

SKETCH

MEASUREMENT

MATERIALS

ITEM	QUANTITY	PRICE
☐		
☐		
☐		
☐		
☐		

PROJECT NAME

PROJECT TYPE ☐ CLOTHING ☐ HOME DECOR ☐ OTHER

SEWING PATTERN

MADE FOR

STARTED

FINISHED

SET-UP

MACHINE

SETTINGS

NEEDLE USED

THREAD USED

SKETCH

MEASUREMENT

MATERIALS

ITEM	QUANTITY	PRICE
☐		
☐		
☐		
☐		
☐		

PROJECT NAME					
PROJECT TYPE	☐ CLOTHING		☐ HOME DECOR		☐ OTHER
SEWING PATTERN			**MADE FOR**		
STARTED			**FINISHED**		

SET-UP

- MACHINE
- SETTINGS
- NEEDLE USED
- THREAD USED

SKETCH

MEASUREMENT

MATERIALS

ITEM	QUANTITY	PRICE
☐		
☐		
☐		
☐		
☐		

PROJECT NAME

PROJECT TYPE ☐ CLOTHING ☐ HOME DECOR ☐ OTHER

SEWING PATTERN | **MADE FOR**

STARTED | **FINISHED**

SET-UP

- MACHINE
- SETTINGS
- NEEDLE USED
- THREAD USED

SKETCH

MEASUREMENT

MATERIALS

ITEM	QUANTITY	PRICE
☐		
☐		
☐		
☐		
☐		

	PROJECT NAME		
PROJECT TYPE	☐ CLOTHING	☐ HOME DECOR	☐ OTHER

SEWING PATTERN	MADE FOR
STARTED	FINISHED

SET-UP

- MACHINE
- SETTINGS
- NEEDLE USED
- THREAD USED

SKETCH

MEASUREMENT

MATERIALS

ITEM	QUANTITY	PRICE
☐		
☐		
☐		
☐		
☐		

PROJECT NAME	
PROJECT TYPE	☐ CLOTHING ☐ HOME DECOR ☐ OTHER

SEWING PATTERN	MADE FOR
STARTED	FINISHED

SET-UP

- MACHINE
- SETTINGS
- NEEDLE USED
- THREAD USED

SKETCH

MEASUREMENT

MATERIALS

ITEM	QUANTITY	PRICE
☐		
☐		
☐		
☐		
☐		

	PROJECT NAME		
PROJECT TYPE	☐ CLOTHING	☐ HOME DECOR	☐ OTHER
SEWING PATTERN		MADE FOR	
STARTED		FINISHED	

SET-UP

- MACHINE
- SETTINGS
- NEEDLE USED
- THREAD USED

SKETCH

MEASUREMENT

MATERIALS

ITEM	QUANTITY	PRICE
☐		
☐		
☐		
☐		
☐		

	PROJECT NAME	
	PROJECT TYPE ☐ CLOTHING ☐ HOME DECOR ☐ OTHER	
	SEWING PATTERN	MADE FOR
	STARTED	FINISHED

SET-UP

- MACHINE
- SETTINGS
- NEEDLE USED
- THREAD USED

SKETCH

MEASUREMENT

MATERIALS

ITEM	QUANTITY	PRICE
☐		
☐		
☐		
☐		
☐		

PROJECT NAME	
PROJECT TYPE	☐ CLOTHING ☐ HOME DECOR ☐ OTHER
SEWING PATTERN	MADE FOR
STARTED	FINISHED

SET-UP

- MACHINE
- SETTINGS
- NEEDLE USED
- THREAD USED

SKETCH

MEASUREMENT

MATERIALS

ITEM	QUANTITY	PRICE
☐		
☐		
☐		
☐		
☐		

PROJECT NAME	
PROJECT TYPE ☐ CLOTHING ☐ HOME DECOR ☐ OTHER	
SEWING PATTERN	MADE FOR
STARTED	FINISHED

SET-UP

MACHINE	
SETTINGS	
NEEDLE USED	
THREAD USED	

SKETCH

MEASUREMENT

MATERIALS

ITEM	QUANTITY	PRICE
☐		
☐		
☐		
☐		
☐		

PROJECT NAME

PROJECT TYPE ☐ CLOTHING ☐ HOME DECOR ☐ OTHER

SEWING PATTERN

MADE FOR

STARTED

FINISHED

SET-UP

- MACHINE
- SETTINGS
- NEEDLE USED
- THREAD USED

MEASUREMENT

SKETCH

MATERIALS

ITEM	QUANTITY	PRICE
☐		
☐		
☐		
☐		
☐		

- **PROJECT NAME**
- **PROJECT TYPE** ☐ CLOTHING   ☐ HOME DECOR   ☐ OTHER
- **SEWING PATTERN**
- **MADE FOR**
- **STARTED**
- **FINISHED**

SET-UP
- MACHINE
- SETTINGS
- NEEDLE USED
- THREAD USED

SKETCH

MEASUREMENT

MATERIALS

ITEM	QUANTITY	PRICE
☐		
☐		
☐		
☐		
☐		

PROJECT NAME					
PROJECT TYPE	☐ CLOTHING		☐ HOME DECOR		☐ OTHER
SEWING PATTERN			MADE FOR		
STARTED			FINISHED		

SET-UP

- MACHINE
- SETTINGS
- NEEDLE USED
- THREAD USED

SKETCH

MEASUREMENT

MATERIALS

ITEM	QUANTITY	PRICE
☐		
☐		
☐		
☐		
☐		

PROJECT NAME	
PROJECT TYPE ☐ CLOTHING ☐ HOME DECOR ☐ OTHER	
SEWING PATTERN	MADE FOR
STARTED	FINISHED

SET-UP

- MACHINE
- SETTINGS
- NEEDLE USED
- THREAD USED

SKETCH

MEASUREMENT

MATERIALS

ITEM	QUANTITY	PRICE
☐		
☐		
☐		
☐		
☐		

PROJECT NAME	

PROJECT TYPE	☐ CLOTHING	☐ HOME DECOR	☐ OTHER

SEWING PATTERN	MADE FOR
STARTED	FINISHED

SET-UP

- MACHINE
- SETTINGS
- NEEDLE USED
- THREAD USED

SKETCH

MEASUREMENT

MATERIALS

ITEM	QUANTITY	PRICE
☐		
☐		
☐		
☐		
☐		

PROJECT NAME	
PROJECT TYPE	☐ CLOTHING ☐ HOME DECOR ☐ OTHER
SEWING PATTERN	MADE FOR
STARTED	FINISHED

SET-UP

- MACHINE
- SETTINGS
- NEEDLE USED
- THREAD USED

SKETCH

MEASUREMENT

MATERIALS

ITEM	QUANTITY	PRICE
☐		
☐		
☐		
☐		
☐		

- PROJECT NAME
- PROJECT TYPE ☐ CLOTHING ☐ HOME DECOR ☐ OTHER
- SEWING PATTERN
- MADE FOR
- STARTED
- FINISHED

SET-UP

- MACHINE
- SETTINGS
- NEEDLE USED
- THREAD USED

SKETCH

MEASUREMENT

MATERIALS

ITEM	QUANTITY	PRICE
☐		
☐		
☐		
☐		
☐		

PROJECT NAME	
PROJECT TYPE	☐ CLOTHING ☐ HOME DECOR ☐ OTHER
SEWING PATTERN	MADE FOR
STARTED	FINISHED

SET-UP

- MACHINE
- SETTINGS
- NEEDLE USED
- THREAD USED

SKETCH

MEASUREMENT

MATERIALS

ITEM	QUANTITY	PRICE
☐		
☐		
☐		
☐		
☐		

PROJECT NAME	
PROJECT TYPE ☐ CLOTHING ☐ HOME DECOR ☐ OTHER	
SEWING PATTERN	MADE FOR
STARTED	FINISHED

SET-UP

- MACHINE
- SETTINGS
- NEEDLE USED
- THREAD USED

SKETCH

MEASUREMENT

MATERIALS

ITEM	QUANTITY	PRICE
☐		
☐		
☐		
☐		
☐		

	PROJECT NAME	
	PROJECT TYPE ☐ CLOTHING ☐ HOME DECOR ☐ OTHER	
	SEWING PATTERN	MADE FOR
	STARTED	FINISHED

SET-UP

- MACHINE
- SETTINGS
- NEEDLE USED
- THREAD USED

SKETCH

MEASUREMENT

MATERIALS

ITEM	QUANTITY	PRICE
☐		
☐		
☐		
☐		
☐		

PROJECT NAME	
PROJECT TYPE ☐ CLOTHING ☐ HOME DECOR ☐ OTHER	
SEWING PATTERN	MADE FOR
STARTED	FINISHED

SET-UP

- MACHINE
- SETTINGS
- NEEDLE USED
- THREAD USED

MEASUREMENT

SKETCH

MATERIALS

ITEM	QUANTITY	PRICE
☐		
☐		
☐		
☐		
☐		

- PROJECT NAME
- PROJECT TYPE ☐ CLOTHING ☐ HOME DECOR ☐ OTHER
- SEWING PATTERN
- MADE FOR
- STARTED
- FINISHED

SET-UP

- MACHINE
- SETTINGS
- NEEDLE USED
- THREAD USED

SKETCH

MEASUREMENT

MATERIALS

ITEM	QUANTITY	PRICE
☐		
☐		
☐		
☐		
☐		

PROJECT NAME

PROJECT TYPE ☐ CLOTHING ☐ HOME DECOR ☐ OTHER

SEWING PATTERN | **MADE FOR**

STARTED | **FINISHED**

SET-UP

- MACHINE
- SETTINGS
- NEEDLE USED
- THREAD USED

SKETCH

MEASUREMENT

MATERIALS

ITEM	QUANTITY	PRICE
☐		
☐		
☐		
☐		
☐		

PROJECT NAME	
PROJECT TYPE ☐ CLOTHING ☐ HOME DECOR ☐ OTHER	
SEWING PATTERN	MADE FOR
STARTED	FINISHED

SET-UP

- MACHINE
- SETTINGS
- NEEDLE USED
- THREAD USED

MEASUREMENT

SKETCH

MATERIALS

ITEM	QUANTITY	PRICE
☐		
☐		
☐		
☐		
☐		

PROJECT NAME	
PROJECT TYPE ☐ CLOTHING ☐ HOME DECOR ☐ OTHER	
SEWING PATTERN	MADE FOR
STARTED	FINISHED

SET-UP

- MACHINE
- SETTINGS
- NEEDLE USED
- THREAD USED

SKETCH

MEASUREMENT

MATERIALS

ITEM	QUANTITY	PRICE
☐		
☐		
☐		
☐		
☐		

	PROJECT NAME		
	PROJECT TYPE ☐ CLOTHING	☐ HOME DECOR	☐ OTHER
	SEWING PATTERN	MADE FOR	
	STARTED	FINISHED	

SET-UP

- MACHINE
- SETTINGS
-
- NEEDLE USED
- THREAD USED

SKETCH

MEASUREMENT

MATERIALS

ITEM	QUANTITY	PRICE
☐		
☐		
☐		
☐		
☐		

PROJECT NAME	
PROJECT TYPE ☐ CLOTHING ☐ HOME DECOR ☐ OTHER	
SEWING PATTERN	MADE FOR
STARTED	FINISHED

SET-UP

- MACHINE
- SETTINGS
- NEEDLE USED
- THREAD USED

SKETCH

MEASUREMENT

MATERIALS

ITEM	QUANTITY	PRICE
☐		
☐		
☐		
☐		
☐		

PROJECT NAME

PROJECT TYPE ☐ CLOTHING   ☐ HOME DECOR   ☐ OTHER

SEWING PATTERN | **MADE FOR**

STARTED | **FINISHED**

SET-UP

- MACHINE
- SETTINGS
- NEEDLE USED
- THREAD USED

SKETCH

MEASUREMENT

MATERIALS

ITEM	QUANTITY	PRICE
☐		
☐		
☐		
☐		
☐		

PROJECT NAME

PROJECT TYPE ☐ CLOTHING ☐ HOME DECOR ☐ OTHER

SEWING PATTERN

MADE FOR

STARTED

FINISHED

SET-UP

- MACHINE
- SETTINGS
- NEEDLE USED
- THREAD USED

SKETCH

MEASUREMENT

MATERIALS

ITEM	QUANTITY	PRICE
☐		
☐		
☐		
☐		
☐		

PROJECT NAME	
PROJECT TYPE ☐ CLOTHING ☐ HOME DECOR ☐ OTHER	
SEWING PATTERN	**MADE FOR**
STARTED	**FINISHED**

SET-UP

- MACHINE
- SETTINGS
- NEEDLE USED
- THREAD USED

SKETCH

MEASUREMENT

MATERIALS

ITEM	QUANTITY	PRICE
☐		
☐		
☐		
☐		
☐		

PROJECT NAME	
PROJECT TYPE ☐ CLOTHING ☐ HOME DECOR ☐ OTHER	
SEWING PATTERN	**MADE FOR**
STARTED	**FINISHED**

SET-UP

- MACHINE
- SETTINGS
- NEEDLE USED
- THREAD USED

SKETCH

MEASUREMENT

MATERIALS

ITEM	QUANTITY	PRICE
☐		
☐		
☐		
☐		
☐		

PROJECT NAME	
PROJECT TYPE ☐ CLOTHING ☐ HOME DECOR ☐ OTHER	
SEWING PATTERN	**MADE FOR**
STARTED	**FINISHED**

SET-UP

MACHINE	
SETTINGS	
NEEDLE USED	
THREAD USED	

SKETCH

MEASUREMENT

MATERIALS

ITEM	QUANTITY	PRICE
☐		
☐		
☐		
☐		
☐		

PROJECT NAME	
PROJECT TYPE ☐ CLOTHING ☐ HOME DECOR ☐ OTHER	
SEWING PATTERN	MADE FOR
STARTED	FINISHED

SET-UP

- MACHINE
- SETTINGS
- NEEDLE USED
- THREAD USED

SKETCH

MEASUREMENT

MATERIALS

ITEM	QUANTITY	PRICE
☐		
☐		
☐		
☐		
☐		

PROJECT NAME

PROJECT TYPE ☐ CLOTHING ☐ HOME DECOR ☐ OTHER

SEWING PATTERN | **MADE FOR**

STARTED | **FINISHED**

SET-UP

- MACHINE
- SETTINGS
- NEEDLE USED
- THREAD USED

SKETCH

MEASUREMENT

MATERIALS

ITEM	QUANTITY	PRICE
☐		
☐		
☐		
☐		
☐		

PROJECT NAME	
PROJECT TYPE ☐ CLOTHING ☐ HOME DECOR ☐ OTHER	
SEWING PATTERN	**MADE FOR**
STARTED	**FINISHED**

SET-UP

MACHINE
SETTINGS
NEEDLE USED
THREAD USED

SKETCH

MEASUREMENT

MATERIALS

ITEM	QUANTITY	PRICE
☐		
☐		
☐		
☐		
☐		

- PROJECT NAME
- PROJECT TYPE ☐ CLOTHING ☐ HOME DECOR ☐ OTHER
- SEWING PATTERN
- MADE FOR
- STARTED
- FINISHED

SET-UP

- MACHINE
- SETTINGS
- NEEDLE USED
- THREAD USED

MEASUREMENT

SKETCH

MATERIALS

ITEM	QUANTITY	PRICE
☐		
☐		
☐		
☐		
☐		

👗 **PROJECT NAME**	

🔘 **PROJECT TYPE**	☐ CLOTHING		☐ HOME DECOR		☐ OTHER

🧥 **SEWING PATTERN**		🎁 **MADE FOR**	
⏱ **STARTED**		🚩 **FINISHED**	

SET-UP

🪡 MACHINE	
🎛 SETTINGS	
🧵 NEEDLE USED	
🧶 THREAD USED	

SKETCH

MEASUREMENT

MATERIALS

🧵 ITEM	🧮 QUANTITY	🏷 PRICE
☐		
☐		
☐		
☐		
☐		

PROJECT NAME	
PROJECT TYPE ☐ CLOTHING ☐ HOME DECOR ☐ OTHER	
SEWING PATTERN	MADE FOR
STARTED	FINISHED

SET-UP

- MACHINE
- SETTINGS
- NEEDLE USED
- THREAD USED

SKETCH

MEASUREMENT

MATERIALS

ITEM	QUANTITY	PRICE
☐		
☐		
☐		
☐		
☐		

PROJECT NAME	
PROJECT TYPE ☐ CLOTHING ☐ HOME DECOR ☐ OTHER	
SEWING PATTERN	MADE FOR
STARTED	FINISHED

SET-UP

- MACHINE
- SETTINGS
-
- NEEDLE USED
- THREAD USED

SKETCH

MEASUREMENT

MATERIALS

ITEM	QUANTITY	PRICE
☐		
☐		
☐		
☐		
☐		

PROJECT NAME	
PROJECT TYPE	☐ CLOTHING ☐ HOME DECOR ☐ OTHER
SEWING PATTERN	MADE FOR
STARTED	FINISHED

SET-UP

- MACHINE
- SETTINGS
- NEEDLE USED
- THREAD USED

SKETCH

MEASUREMENT

MATERIALS

ITEM	QUANTITY	PRICE
☐		
☐		
☐		
☐		
☐		

	PROJECT NAME		
PROJECT TYPE	☐ CLOTHING	☐ HOME DECOR	☐ OTHER
SEWING PATTERN		MADE FOR	
STARTED		FINISHED	

SET-UP

- MACHINE
- SETTINGS
- NEEDLE USED
- THREAD USED

SKETCH

MEASUREMENT

MATERIALS

ITEM	QUANTITY	PRICE
☐		
☐		
☐		
☐		
☐		

PROJECT NAME

PROJECT TYPE ☐ CLOTHING ☐ HOME DECOR ☐ OTHER

SEWING PATTERN	MADE FOR
STARTED	FINISHED

SET-UP

- MACHINE
- SETTINGS

- NEEDLE USED
- THREAD USED

MEASUREMENT

SKETCH

MATERIALS

ITEM	QUANTITY	PRICE
☐		
☐		
☐		
☐		
☐		

PROJECT NAME

PROJECT TYPE ☐ CLOTHING ☐ HOME DECOR ☐ OTHER

SEWING PATTERN | **MADE FOR**

STARTED | **FINISHED**

SET-UP

- MACHINE
- SETTINGS
- NEEDLE USED
- THREAD USED

SKETCH

MEASUREMENT

MATERIALS

ITEM	QUANTITY	PRICE
☐		
☐		
☐		
☐		
☐		

PROJECT NAME	
PROJECT TYPE	☐ CLOTHING ☐ HOME DECOR ☐ OTHER
SEWING PATTERN	MADE FOR
STARTED	FINISHED

SET-UP

- MACHINE
- SETTINGS
-
- NEEDLE USED
- THREAD USED

MEASUREMENT

SKETCH

MATERIALS

ITEM	QUANTITY	PRICE
☐		
☐		
☐		
☐		
☐		

PROJECT NAME

PROJECT TYPE ☐ CLOTHING ☐ HOME DECOR ☐ OTHER

SEWING PATTERN

MADE FOR

STARTED

FINISHED

SET-UP

- MACHINE
- SETTINGS
- NEEDLE USED
- THREAD USED

SKETCH

MEASUREMENT

MATERIALS

ITEM	QUANTITY	PRICE
☐		
☐		
☐		
☐		
☐		

PROJECT NAME	
PROJECT TYPE	☐ CLOTHING ☐ HOME DECOR ☐ OTHER
SEWING PATTERN	MADE FOR
STARTED	FINISHED

SET-UP

- MACHINE
- SETTINGS
- NEEDLE USED
- THREAD USED

SKETCH

MEASUREMENT

MATERIALS

ITEM	QUANTITY	PRICE
☐		
☐		
☐		
☐		
☐		

- **PROJECT NAME**
- **PROJECT TYPE** ☐ CLOTHING ☐ HOME DECOR ☐ OTHER
- **SEWING PATTERN**
- **MADE FOR**
- **STARTED**
- **FINISHED**

SET-UP

- MACHINE
- SETTINGS
- NEEDLE USED
- THREAD USED

SKETCH

MEASUREMENT

MATERIALS

ITEM	QUANTITY	PRICE
☐		
☐		
☐		
☐		
☐		

PROJECT NAME

PROJECT TYPE ☐ CLOTHING ☐ HOME DECOR ☐ OTHER

SEWING PATTERN | **MADE FOR**

STARTED | **FINISHED**

SET-UP

- MACHINE
- SETTINGS
- NEEDLE USED
- THREAD USED

SKETCH

MEASUREMENT

MATERIALS

ITEM	QUANTITY	PRICE
☐		
☐		
☐		
☐		
☐		

PROJECT NAME				
PROJECT TYPE	☐ CLOTHING	☐ HOME DECOR		☐ OTHER
SEWING PATTERN		**MADE FOR**		
STARTED		**FINISHED**		

SET-UP

- MACHINE
- SETTINGS
- NEEDLE USED
- THREAD USED

SKETCH

MEASUREMENT

MATERIALS

ITEM	QUANTITY	PRICE
☐		
☐		
☐		
☐		
☐		

PROJECT NAME						
PROJECT TYPE	☐ CLOTHING		☐ HOME DECOR		☐ OTHER	
SEWING PATTERN			**MADE FOR**			
STARTED			**FINISHED**			

SET-UP

- MACHINE
- SETTINGS
- NEEDLE USED
- THREAD USED

SKETCH

MEASUREMENT

MATERIALS

ITEM	QUANTITY	PRICE
☐		
☐		
☐		
☐		
☐		

PROJECT NAME	
PROJECT TYPE	☐ CLOTHING ☐ HOME DECOR ☐ OTHER
SEWING PATTERN	MADE FOR
STARTED	FINISHED

SET-UP

- MACHINE
- SETTINGS
- NEEDLE USED
- THREAD USED

SKETCH

MEASUREMENT

MATERIALS

ITEM	QUANTITY	PRICE
☐		
☐		
☐		
☐		
☐		

- PROJECT NAME
- PROJECT TYPE ☐ CLOTHING ☐ HOME DECOR ☐ OTHER
- SEWING PATTERN
- MADE FOR
- STARTED
- FINISHED

SET-UP

- MACHINE
- SETTINGS
- NEEDLE USED
- THREAD USED

SKETCH

MEASUREMENT

MATERIALS

ITEM	QUANTITY	PRICE
☐		
☐		
☐		
☐		
☐		

PROJECT NAME	
PROJECT TYPE ☐ CLOTHING ☐ HOME DECOR ☐ OTHER	
SEWING PATTERN	MADE FOR
STARTED	FINISHED

SET-UP

- MACHINE
- SETTINGS
- NEEDLE USED
- THREAD USED

SKETCH

MEASUREMENT

MATERIALS

ITEM	QUANTITY	PRICE
☐		
☐		
☐		
☐		
☐		

PROJECT NAME

PROJECT TYPE ☐ CLOTHING ☐ HOME DECOR ☐ OTHER

SEWING PATTERN

MADE FOR

STARTED

FINISHED

SET-UP

MACHINE

SETTINGS

NEEDLE USED

THREAD USED

SKETCH

MEASUREMENT

MATERIALS

ITEM	QUANTITY	PRICE
☐		
☐		
☐		
☐		
☐		

PROJECT NAME	
PROJECT TYPE ☐ CLOTHING ☐ HOME DECOR ☐ OTHER	
SEWING PATTERN	MADE FOR
STARTED	FINISHED

SET-UP

- MACHINE
- SETTINGS
- NEEDLE USED
- THREAD USED

SKETCH

MEASUREMENT

MATERIALS

ITEM	QUANTITY	PRICE
☐		
☐		
☐		
☐		
☐		

PROJECT NAME						
PROJECT TYPE	☐ CLOTHING		☐ HOME DECOR		☐ OTHER	
SEWING PATTERN			**MADE FOR**			
STARTED			**FINISHED**			

SET-UP

- MACHINE
- SETTINGS
- NEEDLE USED
- THREAD USED

SKETCH

MEASUREMENT

MATERIALS

ITEM	QUANTITY	PRICE
☐		
☐		
☐		
☐		
☐		

PROJECT NAME	
PROJECT TYPE ☐ CLOTHING ☐ HOME DECOR ☐ OTHER	
SEWING PATTERN	MADE FOR
STARTED	FINISHED

SET-UP

- MACHINE
- SETTINGS
- NEEDLE USED
- THREAD USED

SKETCH

MEASUREMENT

MATERIALS

ITEM	QUANTITY	PRICE
☐		
☐		
☐		
☐		
☐		

- **PROJECT NAME**
- **PROJECT TYPE** ☐ CLOTHING ☐ HOME DECOR ☐ OTHER
- **SEWING PATTERN**
- **MADE FOR**
- **STARTED**
- **FINISHED**

SET-UP

- MACHINE
- SETTINGS
- NEEDLE USED
- THREAD USED

SKETCH

MEASUREMENT

MATERIALS

ITEM	QUANTITY	PRICE
☐		
☐		
☐		
☐		
☐		

	PROJECT NAME			
	PROJECT TYPE	☐ CLOTHING	☐ HOME DECOR	☐ OTHER
	SEWING PATTERN		MADE FOR	
	STARTED		FINISHED	

SET-UP

- MACHINE
- SETTINGS
- NEEDLE USED
- THREAD USED

SKETCH

MEASUREMENT

MATERIALS

ITEM	QUANTITY	PRICE
☐		
☐		
☐		
☐		
☐		

PROJECT NAME	
PROJECT TYPE ☐ CLOTHING ☐ HOME DECOR ☐ OTHER	
SEWING PATTERN	MADE FOR
STARTED	FINISHED

SET-UP

- MACHINE
- SETTINGS
- NEEDLE USED
- THREAD USED

SKETCH

MEASUREMENT

MATERIALS

ITEM	QUANTITY	PRICE
☐		
☐		
☐		
☐		
☐		

PROJECT NAME

PROJECT TYPE ☐ CLOTHING   ☐ HOME DECOR   ☐ OTHER

SEWING PATTERN | **MADE FOR**

STARTED | **FINISHED**

SET-UP

- MACHINE
- SETTINGS
- NEEDLE USED
- THREAD USED

SKETCH

MEASUREMENT

MATERIALS

ITEM	QUANTITY	PRICE
☐		
☐		
☐		
☐		
☐		

PROJECT NAME

PROJECT TYPE ☐ CLOTHING ☐ HOME DECOR ☐ OTHER

SEWING PATTERN

MADE FOR

STARTED

FINISHED

SET-UP

- MACHINE
- SETTINGS
- NEEDLE USED
- THREAD USED

SKETCH

MEASUREMENT

MATERIALS

ITEM	QUANTITY	PRICE
☐		
☐		
☐		
☐		
☐		

PROJECT NAME				
PROJECT TYPE	☐ CLOTHING	☐ HOME DECOR		☐ OTHER
SEWING PATTERN		MADE FOR		
STARTED		FINISHED		

SET-UP

- MACHINE
- SETTINGS
- NEEDLE USED
- THREAD USED

SKETCH

MEASUREMENT

MATERIALS

ITEM	QUANTITY	PRICE
☐		
☐		
☐		
☐		
☐		

PROJECT NAME	
PROJECT TYPE ☐ CLOTHING ☐ HOME DECOR ☐ OTHER	
SEWING PATTERN	MADE FOR
STARTED	FINISHED

SET-UP

- MACHINE
- SETTINGS
- NEEDLE USED
- THREAD USED

MEASUREMENT

SKETCH

MATERIALS

ITEM	QUANTITY	PRICE
☐		
☐		
☐		
☐		
☐		

PROJECT NAME	

PROJECT TYPE	☐ CLOTHING		☐ HOME DECOR		☐ OTHER

SEWING PATTERN	MADE FOR
STARTED	FINISHED

SET-UP

- MACHINE
- SETTINGS
- NEEDLE USED
- THREAD USED

SKETCH

MEASUREMENT

MATERIALS

ITEM	QUANTITY	PRICE
☐		
☐		
☐		
☐		
☐		

- PROJECT NAME
- PROJECT TYPE ☐ CLOTHING ☐ HOME DECOR ☐ OTHER
- SEWING PATTERN
- MADE FOR
- STARTED
- FINISHED

SET-UP

- MACHINE
- SETTINGS
- NEEDLE USED
- THREAD USED

SKETCH

MEASUREMENT

MATERIALS

ITEM	QUANTITY	PRICE
☐		
☐		
☐		
☐		
☐		

PROJECT NAME	
PROJECT TYPE ☐ CLOTHING ☐ HOME DECOR ☐ OTHER	
SEWING PATTERN	MADE FOR
STARTED	FINISHED

SET-UP

- MACHINE
- SETTINGS
- NEEDLE USED
- THREAD USED

SKETCH

MEASUREMENT

MATERIALS

ITEM	QUANTITY	PRICE
☐		
☐		
☐		
☐		
☐		

PROJECT NAME	
PROJECT TYPE ☐ CLOTHING ☐ HOME DECOR ☐ OTHER	
SEWING PATTERN	**MADE FOR**
STARTED	**FINISHED**

SET-UP

- MACHINE
- SETTINGS
- NEEDLE USED
- THREAD USED

SKETCH

MEASUREMENT

MATERIALS

ITEM	QUANTITY	PRICE
☐		
☐		
☐		
☐		
☐		

PROJECT NAME	
PROJECT TYPE ☐ CLOTHING ☐ HOME DECOR ☐ OTHER	
SEWING PATTERN	MADE FOR
STARTED	FINISHED

SET-UP

- MACHINE
- SETTINGS
- NEEDLE USED
- THREAD USED

MEASUREMENT

SKETCH

MATERIALS

ITEM	QUANTITY	PRICE
☐		
☐		
☐		
☐		
☐		

PROJECT NAME

PROJECT TYPE ☐ CLOTHING ☐ HOME DECOR ☐ OTHER

SEWING PATTERN

MADE FOR

STARTED

FINISHED

SET-UP

- MACHINE
- SETTINGS
- NEEDLE USED
- THREAD USED

SKETCH

MEASUREMENT

MATERIALS

ITEM	QUANTITY	PRICE
☐		
☐		
☐		
☐		
☐		

PROJECT NAME	
PROJECT TYPE ☐ CLOTHING ☐ HOME DECOR ☐ OTHER	
SEWING PATTERN	MADE FOR
STARTED	FINISHED

SET-UP

- MACHINE
- SETTINGS
- NEEDLE USED
- THREAD USED

SKETCH

MEASUREMENT

MATERIALS

ITEM	QUANTITY	PRICE
☐		
☐		
☐		
☐		
☐		

PROJECT NAME

PROJECT TYPE ☐ CLOTHING   ☐ HOME DECOR   ☐ OTHER

SEWING PATTERN | **MADE FOR**

STARTED | **FINISHED**

SET-UP

- MACHINE
- SETTINGS
- NEEDLE USED
- THREAD USED

SKETCH

MEASUREMENT

MATERIALS

ITEM	QUANTITY	PRICE
☐		
☐		
☐		
☐		
☐		

PROJECT NAME	
PROJECT TYPE ☐ CLOTHING ☐ HOME DECOR ☐ OTHER	
SEWING PATTERN	MADE FOR
STARTED	FINISHED

SET-UP

- MACHINE
- SETTINGS
- NEEDLE USED
- THREAD USED

SKETCH

MEASUREMENT

MATERIALS

ITEM	QUANTITY	PRICE
☐		
☐		
☐		
☐		
☐		

PROJECT NAME	
PROJECT TYPE ☐ CLOTHING ☐ HOME DECOR ☐ OTHER	
SEWING PATTERN	MADE FOR
STARTED	FINISHED

SET-UP

- MACHINE
- SETTINGS
-
- NEEDLE USED
- THREAD USED

SKETCH

MEASUREMENT

MATERIALS

ITEM	QUANTITY	PRICE
☐		
☐		
☐		
☐		
☐		

PROJECT NAME

PROJECT TYPE ☐ CLOTHING ☐ HOME DECOR ☐ OTHER

SEWING PATTERN	MADE FOR
STARTED	FINISHED

SET-UP

- MACHINE
- SETTINGS
- NEEDLE USED
- THREAD USED

SKETCH

MEASUREMENT

MATERIALS

ITEM	QUANTITY	PRICE
☐		
☐		
☐		
☐		
☐		

PROJECT NAME	

PROJECT TYPE	☐ CLOTHING		☐ HOME DECOR		☐ OTHER

SEWING PATTERN		MADE FOR	
STARTED		FINISHED	

SET-UP

- MACHINE
- SETTINGS
- NEEDLE USED
- THREAD USED

SKETCH

MEASUREMENT

MATERIALS

ITEM	QUANTITY	PRICE
☐		
☐		
☐		
☐		
☐		

PROJECT NAME	

PROJECT TYPE	☐ CLOTHING		☐ HOME DECOR		☐ OTHER

SEWING PATTERN	MADE FOR
STARTED	FINISHED

SET-UP

- MACHINE
- SETTINGS
- NEEDLE USED
- THREAD USED

SKETCH

MEASUREMENT

MATERIALS

ITEM	QUANTITY	PRICE
☐		
☐		
☐		
☐		
☐		

- PROJECT NAME
- PROJECT TYPE ☐ CLOTHING ☐ HOME DECOR ☐ OTHER
- SEWING PATTERN
- MADE FOR
- STARTED
- FINISHED

SET-UP

- MACHINE
- SETTINGS
- NEEDLE USED
- THREAD USED

SKETCH

MEASUREMENT

MATERIALS

ITEM	QUANTITY	PRICE
☐		
☐		
☐		
☐		
☐		

PROJECT NAME	

PROJECT TYPE	☐ CLOTHING	☐ HOME DECOR	☐ OTHER

SEWING PATTERN	MADE FOR
STARTED	FINISHED

SET-UP

- MACHINE
- SETTINGS
-
- NEEDLE USED
- THREAD USED

SKETCH

MEASUREMENT

MATERIALS

ITEM	QUANTITY	PRICE
☐		
☐		
☐		
☐		
☐		

PROJECT NAME

PROJECT TYPE ☐ CLOTHING ☐ HOME DECOR ☐ OTHER

SEWING PATTERN

MADE FOR

STARTED

FINISHED

SET-UP

MACHINE

SETTINGS

NEEDLE USED

THREAD USED

SKETCH

MEASUREMENT

MATERIALS

ITEM	QUANTITY	PRICE
☐		
☐		
☐		
☐		
☐		

PROJECT NAME

PROJECT TYPE ☐ CLOTHING ☐ HOME DECOR ☐ OTHER

SEWING PATTERN

MADE FOR

STARTED

FINISHED

SET-UP

- MACHINE
- SETTINGS
- NEEDLE USED
- THREAD USED

SKETCH

MEASUREMENT

MATERIALS

ITEM	QUANTITY	PRICE
☐		
☐		
☐		
☐		
☐		

PROJECT NAME

PROJECT TYPE ☐ CLOTHING ☐ HOME DECOR ☐ OTHER

SEWING PATTERN | **MADE FOR**

STARTED | **FINISHED**

SET-UP

- MACHINE
- SETTINGS
- NEEDLE USED
- THREAD USED

SKETCH

MEASUREMENT

MATERIALS

ITEM	QUANTITY	PRICE
☐		
☐		
☐		
☐		
☐		

PROJECT NAME

PROJECT TYPE ☐ CLOTHING ☐ HOME DECOR ☐ OTHER

SEWING PATTERN | **MADE FOR**

STARTED | **FINISHED**

SET-UP

- MACHINE
- SETTINGS
- NEEDLE USED
- THREAD USED

SKETCH

MEASUREMENT

MATERIALS

ITEM	QUANTITY	PRICE
☐		
☐		
☐		
☐		
☐		

Printed in Great Britain
by Amazon